DOWN ELSWICK SLIP

ARMSTRONG'S SHIPS AND PEOPLE

1884-1918

'… *an inspection of our places of industry which omits a view of the Elswick Works is rather like the play of Hamlet with the part of the Prince left out.*'

Sir William Armstrong, in a speech to the Prince of Wales, 1884

Dick Keys and Ken Smith

Published by Newcastle City Libraries

Photographic acknowledgements:

Photographs and illustrations are copyright of Newcastle City Libraries except for those on pages:
19, 45, reproduced courtesy of Dick Keys;
4, reproduced courtesy of Tyne & Wear Archives;
17, 37, reproduced courtesy of Tyne & Wear Museums.
The drawing of HMS *Wasp* on page 38 is by Dick Keys.

Reproductions of photographs in this book, for which Newcastle City Libraries hold copyright, may be ordered from the Central Library, Local Studies Section.

Ken Smith is co-author of *Swans of the Tyne: a Pictorial Tribute to Tyne Shipbuilders Swan Hunter*, and *Built With Pride: Tyne Ships 1969-1994*, both published by Newcastle City Libraries.

The authors wish to thank Pat Cook for her work in preparing the manuscript, and West Newcastle Local Studies for their help with research.

Front cover:

An impressive stern view of the battleship *Victoria* on the stocks at the Elswick yard in 1887. Her propellers are waiting for more blades to be fitted.

Back cover:

The founder, Sir William Armstrong (front in top hat), at the launch of the cruiser *Pandora* in August 1889. The *Pandora* was renamed *Katoomba* and served on the Royal Navy's Australian Station until 1905.

CONTENTS

ILLUSTRATIONS

Elswick from King's Meadows, with _Panther_ on the stocks.

A view of the Elswick Shipyard taken circa early 1885. The yard had opened for production the previous year and its first ship, the torpedo cruiser _Panther_, can be seen on the stocks. The _Panther_, built for the Austro-Hungarian Navy, was launched in June 1885. Three months later a sister ship, the _Leopard_, was also launched from the yard.

This photograph was taken from King's Meadows island in the river. The island was an obstacle to navigation and was soon to be dredged away by the Tyne Improvement Commission. The ship on the left is the Chilean ironclad _Blanco Encalada_, which was undergoing a refit. In 1891 she became one of the first vessels to be sunk by torpedo.

A Shipyard at Elswick

On Saturday 13 June 1885 the Austro-Hungarian torpedo cruiser *Panther* became the first ship to be launched from the Elswick Yard in Newcastle. Thousands of spectators turned out to witness the vessel's birth. From early afternoon the wives, children and friends of the workmen, as well as a substantial proportion of Elswick's population, thronged into the yard. Every vantage point was occupied and another crowd lined the opposite bank of the Tyne to gain a view of the warship entering the water.

Just after 3.30pm the last impeding chocks were knocked clear. Lady Armstrong sent a bottle of champagne shattering against the *Panther*'s bow and then, in the words of the *Newcastle Daily Chronicle*'s reporter, 'she glided smoothly down the ways, dipped into the water, and swam gracefully into midstream. Elegant in shape, and buoyant as a ship, the vessel was a sight calculated to delight the heart of a shipwright'.

The newly-created Elswick Shipyard in the West End of Newcastle was part of William Armstrong's great Elswick Works which he had founded in 1847 to manufacture hydraulic equipment. The most important products in the early years of the works included Armstrong's hydraulic crane, but later the pioneering industrialist and inventor moved into the field of armaments, making Elswick one of the largest gun-manufacturing complexes in the world. Former artillery officer and gun expert Andrew Noble played a leading role in this development and became a partner in the business.

The company met with a great deal of success and William Armstrong was knighted, later becoming the 1st Lord Armstrong of Cragside. In due course, Andrew Noble also received a knighthood.

Armstrong turned his attention to plans for producing naval guns and came to an agreement with Charles Mitchell who owned a shipbuilding yard at Low Walker in the East End of Newcastle. Mitchell's yard agreed to build warships and Armstrong's Elswick Works to manufacture the guns for them. The first vessel to result from this joint enterprise was the gunboat *Staunch*, delivered in 1868.

The completion of the Swing Bridge between Newcastle and Gateshead in 1876 began a new era in Tyneside's industrial history. Hitherto, a low eighteenth century stone bridge had barred the passage of ships to and from the upper reaches of the Tyne where Armstrong's works were situated. The demolition of this attractive but problematic structure and its replacement with the Swing Bridge, with its ability to open to let ships pass, meant the industrial development of the western half of Newcastle and Gateshead could accelerate. This was also helped by dredging and the removal of other impediments to navigation carried out by the Tyne Improvement Commission. The iron superstructure and machinery of the new bridge were built by Armstrong's company. The remainder was the work of the Tyne Improvement Commission, which paid for the cost of the entire project. The scene was thus set for warships to be built at Elswick, twelve miles from the sea.

In November 1882 the firms of Armstrong and Mitchell agreed to merge. It was planned that most of the new company's warship production would be transferred to Elswick, with the Low Walker yard concentrating mainly on merchant vessels. The firm took the name Sir W.G. Armstrong Mitchell and Co. Ltd.

The new Elswick Shipyard was situated to the south of Scotswood Road and almost immediately to the west of Water Street. Its site corresponds approximately to the present day Hampshire Court and the eastern sections of Monarch Road

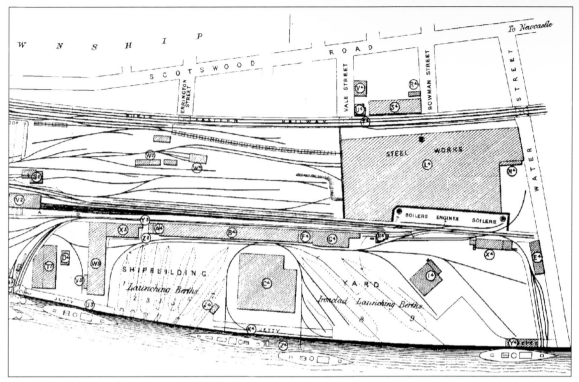

*The Elswick Shipyard in 1886, taken from a brochure entitled 'A Visit to the Works of Sir W.G. Armstrong, Mitchell & Co. Ltd., Elswick, August 1886'. On the stocks were HMS **Renown,** (later **Victoria**) the **Rattler** and the **Wasp.***

in 1905 that Elswick vessels made their most dramatic impact upon the world stage. Tsushima was the decisive naval engagement of the Russo-Japanese War. At this clash in the seas separating Japan and Korea, the Russian Baltic Fleet suffered a crushing defeat. The victorious Japanese ships were commanded by Admiral Heihachiro Togo. Many of the Japanese fleet's guns were supplied by the Elswick Works and four of Togo's cruisers in the battle, the *Asama, Iwate, Idzumo* and *Tokiwa,* had been built at Elswick. Three cruisers launched at the company's Low Walker yard, the *Idzumi, Naniwa* and *Takachiho,* also took part. However, it should be noted that cruisers built at Low Walker are sometimes referred to as 'Elswick cruisers', an understandable confusion.

and Amethyst Road, now part of a business park. There were nine building berths, laid out on either side of a steel plate workshop.

The opening of the yard in 1884 heralded the start of an extraordinary chapter in Tyneside's history. Austria-Hungary was the first of many nations to place orders for warships, including Britain, Japan, China, Argentina, Chile, Brazil, Norway, Portugal, Spain, Italy, Turkey and Rumania. In addition, the United States purchased two vessels originally intended for service with the Brazilian Navy.

Among the most prominent customers was the Imperial Japanese Navy, which took delivery of nine ships from the yard between 1893 and 1906. It was at the Battle of Tsushima

Low Walker's *Idzumi* had originally been constructed for the Chilean Navy in 1883-84 under the name *Esmeralda* and was the first of the company's so-called 'protected' cruisers. These ships were fast and relatively well-protected by the standards of the day, but from the late 1890s onwards the company began to launch more heavily armoured cruisers, such as the *Asama* and *Tokiwa.* By this time Elswick cruisers had become internationally renowned and for much of its life the yard specialised in this type of vessel. They included a second *Esmeralda,* launched for Chile in 1896.

Between 1885 and 1918 a total of ninety armed ships were launched at the yard including battleships. One of the more unusual vessels was a royal yacht for the Sultan of Turkey, the

Erthogroul (see page 35). The list also included submarines.

But it was the torpedo cruiser *Panther* which began it all. Her keel was laid down on 1 October 1884. At the time the yard was far from complete, so ship and yard took shape together. On her trials off Tynemouth the following year she achieved a speed of over 18 knots. It was a very creditable performance.

As well as being the first Elswick-built warship, the *Panther* was also one of the first torpedo cruisers. This class of vessel was produced in reaction to a proliferation in the numbers of torpedo boats during the 1880s. Fast, armed with a deadly weapon, they caused considerable anxiety among naval authorities throughout the world who had visions of their capital ships being overwhelmed by swarms of these little craft. One of the solutions to the problem was to have a vessel better armed and with the speed to pursue and sink any offending torpedo boat.

The *Panther* was delivered to the Austro-Hungarian Navy complete and ready for sea except for her armament and warlike stores. Paradoxically, while Armstrong Mitchell's ranked amongst the world's foremost armament manufacturers, the contract to supply the guns for the first warship to be built at their new yard went to their arch-rival, Krupps of Essen. These were put aboard when she arrived at Pola in the Adriatic, then a base for her country's navy.

Although when first completed the ship was considered

First ship from the Elswick Yard. The Austro-Hungarian torpedo cruiser **Panther**, launched in 1885.

fast, it was not long before a new generation of torpedo boats eclipsed her capabilities. Unable to match their speed, the *Panther* soon became inadequate for the purpose for which she had been designed. But despite this early obsolescence she served the Austro-Hungarian Navy for thirty-five years.

The end of the First World War also led to the end of Austria-Hungary as a country and to the dissolution of its navy. Under the terms of the Treaty of St Germain the *Panther* was ceded to Britain, but she never returned to the country of her birth. Instead, in 1922, she was sold to shipbreakers in Messina, Italy.

Spanish sisters

The cruisers *Isla de Luzon* and *Isla de Cuba* alongside at the Elswick Yard. Both launched within a month of one another in 1886, they were scuttled by the Americans at the Battle of Manila Bay in the Philippines during the Spanish-American War of 1898. However, after the war the sisters were raised, repaired and incorporated into the United States Navy.

The *Isla de Cuba* was sold to the Venezuelan government in 1912, becoming the *Mariscal Sucre* and did not go to the breakers until 1940. The *Isla de Luzon* was sold to a private company in 1920 who renamed her *Reviver* and intended to make her a salvage vessel, but engine problems put an end to this plan and she was broken up in 1931.

Workers and Dignitaries

In 1897 Lord Armstrong's company underwent another transformation when it amalgamated with the Manchester-based firm of Sir Joseph Whitworth and became known as Sir W.G. Armstrong Whitworth and Co. Ltd. Lord Armstrong died in 1900 and was succeeded as chairman by Sir Andrew Noble.

By 1886 the Elswick Works was employing up to 12,000 people and by 1906 this figure had reached 23,000 when working to full capacity. The works dominated the economy of Newcastle's West End and there can have been few families in the terraced rows of the district which did not have at least one member working for Armstrong Whitworth. The company also opened a works at nearby Scotswood which specialised in producing shot, shells and fuses.

High-ranking naval officers and representatives of foreign governments came to the shipyard to witness launches and to take delivery of vessels. Dignitaries also arrived to tour the works, not least of them the victorious Admiral Togo of Japan who in 1911 stayed as a guest of Sir Andrew Noble at his home, Jesmond Dene House in Jesmond Dene Road, Newcastle. The admiral was accompanied by his A.D.C., Commander N. Taniguchi, and Commander E. Saito.

Togo, one of the few foreigners to hold Britain's Order of Merit, spent a full day at Elswick, arriving at the Water Street entrance of the works with his staff shortly after 10am. He was given a guided tour by three directors who first took him to the steelworks and ordnance department.

The quiet but charismatic admiral saw guns in various stages of manufacture and was also shown models of some of the ships built for the Imperial Japanese Navy. These included the *Naniwa* (sometimes referred to as the *Naniwa Kan*), which Togo had commanded, and the battleship *Hatsuse*. After the models came the real vessels. The party were taken to the shipyard where they boarded HMS *Monarch*, a battleship in the

Admiral Togo during his visit to Newcastle in 1911. Left to right, Admiral W.C. Dundas, Admiral Togo (seated), Sir Andrew Noble, Commander S. Saito, Lady Noble and Commander N. Taniguchi. The photograph was taken at Sir Andrew's home, Jesmond Dene House.

process of being fitted out. This vessel had been launched from the yard in March of that year. The admiral and his staff then went on to inspect the cruiser HMS *Weymouth*, which had recently completed her trials.

After lunch was served, the guests visited various workshops where messages of welcome were displayed. The *Newcastle Illustrated Chronicle* reported: 'In the forge tools and castings had been arranged on the floor forming the words "Welcome to Admiral Togo, O.M.". That the admiral appreciated the welcome thus extended to him was shown by the deep interest he took in everything round about, and the trouble he took to examine the minute details.'

Next, the visitors were taken by motor cars to Scotswood where they saw 13.5-inch shells being made. They then toured Armstrong Whitworth's motor car production section. Togo and his entourage returned to Elswick for tea at 5pm.

During his three-day stay in Newcastle the admiral was also received by the Lord Mayor and took a trip down the Tyne in a steam launch.

Among the many other VIPs to visit the shipyard and works was Winston Churchill, who arrived in October 1913 in his capacity as First Lord of the Admiralty. Churchill spent part of his visit aboard the Admiralty yacht *Enchantress,* which was moored in the river. Accompanied by Rear Admiral Moore and General Sir Ian Hamilton he toured the yard, steelworks and ordnance factory.

The man destined to become Britain's Prime Minister during the Second World War inspected the battleship *Rio de Janeiro*, which had been ordered by the Brazilian Navy but which was later sold to Turkey, only to be seized by Britain on the outbreak of war in 1914 and renamed HMS *Agincourt*.

He went on to visit other Tyne yards, including the newly-opened Walker Naval Yard in Newcastle's East End, which was to eventually replace Elswick as Armstrong's shipbuilding base on the river. A tour was also made of the St Peter's Works of Hawthorn Leslie and Co. Ltd., which constructed some of the engines for Elswick ships.

But behind the much publicised official visits of dignitaries and the launching ceremonies lay the realities of shipbuilding life with its hard work, pressures and considerable dangers. The risk of accident was always present and lives could be lost.

For example, a fatal accident occurred during the building of the battleship *Hatsuse* in 1899-1901. Donald McMillan, of Frank Street, Benwell, was working on scaffolding erected about the ship's hull. It was a frosty day and this had made the planking extremely slippery. A loose board had been carelessly lying on top of the planks. It was a lethal combination and Donald McMillan tripped over the board, slipped and plummeted to his death some 30ft below.

Another tragedy occurred during the fitting out of the Chinese cruiser *Chih Yuan* in 1887. A caulker named Thomas Malloy was cutting a hole in the forward bulkhead of the stokehold. His workplace was dark, enclosed and badly ventilated. It only needed an infusion of coal gas to make it a death trap. That is what happened as the unfortunate Thomas Malloy carried out his task. He was found collapsed after being overcome by the fumes and died soon afterwards in the Newcastle Infirmary. An inquest was held at the Durham Ox Inn. The jury returned a verdict of 'Death through coal gas poisoning'.

A gruesome accident occurred in August 1897 shortly before the new Japanese battleship *Yashima* (pictured on page 27) sailed from the Tyne. She had been brought down from Elswick to moorings off Jarrow Slake. Last-minute adjustments to her machinery were being made. One of the hydraulic ammunition hoists leading to the upper deck had been causing some trouble and three fitters were detailed to check it over. One of them remained below while his two workmates climbed to the upper deck to give the apparatus a trial run. When all was ready he shouted: 'Heave up!' The mechanism was set in motion. As the hoist came into view the horrified men above found themselves looking at their workmate's decapitated head.

Jarrow Slake was also the scene of another accident connected with an Elswick-built ship. In October 1889 the completed Italian cruiser *Piemonte* was moored there and not far away the Tyne wherry *Fanny*, carrying gunpowder and ammunition for the ship, also lay moored. Suddenly there was an explosion, followed by other blasts and the *Fanny* erupted into flames. Shells were exploding. The little wherry's skipper, Edward Lowrie, jumped overboard and swam clear along with the skipper of another wherry which had been visiting. Those whose reactions were slower were not so fortunate. One man was killed and two others badly burnt. Among the injured was an official from the Elswick Works and a 15-year-old boy. Miraculously the wood-built *Fanny* remained afloat, an exploding menace to all about. Eventually, an unnamed hero managed to scuttle her.

As soon as they heard the explosions the Italians aboard the *Piemonte* lost no time in sending a boat to give assistance to the vessel's men. The injured were taken off and given first aid by a doctor called from the nearby floating quarantine hospital. Two days after the *Fanny* incident, the newly-completed *Piemonte* left the Tyne for the Italian naval base at La Spezia.

The following year it was a boiler which caused trouble. While the cruiser *Pandora*, later to be known as the *Katoomba*, was fitting out at the yard in September 1890, sixteen men received burns. It happened as the ship's boilers were undergoing their initial tests. Two had been lit, and to promote the better circulation of water a few tubes had been removed. Suddenly, flames rushed out from the ashpit of one of the boilers, enveloping workmen nearby. Most of the burns were superficial and after treatment at the Infirmary the victims were able to return home, except for one unfortunate man who was seriously hurt.

The *Katoomba* was one of five warships built at Elswick especially for service on the Royal Navy's Australian Station. She served in Australian waters until 1905.

Workers at the Elswick Shipyard, 1912.

Strike and Lockout

In 1871 the Elswick Works were gripped by a major strike when the engineers battled to obtain a nine-hour day. After a five-month struggle against the employers, who strongly opposed the demand, they were successful.

The nine-hour day was first conceded in Sunderland, but the workers in Newcastle and Gateshead came up against a determined resistance by the employers who had retaliated to the strike by bringing in foreign workers. However, the engineers persuaded many of these men to return home. The striking members of the Amalgamated Society of Engineers as well as some non-union workers received financial aid from the Northumberland Miners Union. The men were led by John Burnett, who later became general secretary of the Amalgamated Engineers. Delegates from Britain were sent abroad to warn workers in Belgium, Holland, Denmark and Germany against helping the employers by emigration to Tyneside and other areas of the North.

The Times of 11 September 1871 commented: 'If Sir William Armstrong could have retained his Prussian and Danish labourers, he might have laughed at the strike; but Prussians, Danes and English have all succumbed to the pressure of working class opinion in the North … The foreign hands excuse themselves by declaring that they were entrapped into engagements with the Newcastle and Gateshead firms on false pretences, but when there are dealings of this delicate nature between English firms and foreign workmen we must not be astonished if occasional misunderstandings arise. In fact, the foreigners are only following the example of English workmen who were brought to Newcastle before them, and who have since made their escape from their engagements as speedily as possible. A few prosecutions of foreign workmen for breach of contract have been attempted; but this method is scarcely likely to serve the masters in attracting or retaining foreign labour.'

The Times went on to advance a persuasive argument in favour of shorter working hours: 'We do not approve the general policy of trades unions and are decidedly opposed to their methods of action, but we could wish to see other ground chosen for resisting the aggression of the unions than a bare opposition to the Nine Hours Movement. It is alleged, and we believe it, that the engineering trade in the North of England is now most prosperous, and that the masters are making very large profits. If it be reasonable that workmen should from time to time obtain a share in the augmented profits of a business, there is certainly no way in which they could more profitably claim this advantage than in a decrease of the hours of labour. On moral and sanitary grounds short hours of work are desirable, and, so far as industrial interests are concerned, it may be taken for granted that they would gain rather than lose by the further limitation of working hours.' The newspaper added that there were 'very strong physiological and practical arguments' to support the demand that skilled workmen should not be asked to work more than fifty-four hours in a week. It was 'very doubtful whether masters gain anything by exacting longer working hours'.

However, although the employers had given way to the workers' demand in 1871, a second dispute, from July 1897 to January 1898, ended in defeat for the trade unionists. This struggle was over a demand for the eight-hour day and again involved the Amalgamated Engineers. On Tyneside, the industrial battle began with a lockout of workers which had been imposed nationally by the Engineering Employers' Federation, an organisation which appears to have been determined to crush the trade unionists. The masters had taken their action in

Workers make their way up Water Street from the entrance to the Elswick Works Shipyard. They have been on night shift and are heading towards Scotswood Road. The eastern boundary of the works is marked by the high-walled buildings on the right.

response to a strike in London for the eight-hour day. On 13 July 1897 all men employed on day shifts in Tyneside workshops owned by members of the employers' federation ceased work. The masters had given notice to twenty-five per cent of the men and the remaining seventy-five per cent retaliated by sending in their notices to finish at the same time. It was a clear expression of solidarity.

The *Newcastle Daily Journal* reported the following day: 'Contrary to public expectations there was no demonstration when the men left work at 5 o'clock. At Elswick, at Hawthorn Leslie and at Stephenson's the men came out without any sign of being finished for an indefinite period.'

It was estimated that about 9,000 engineers on the North East Coast were affected by the dispute, including 3,500 in Newcastle and Gateshead. Around 15,000 workers in kindred trades were thrown idle. The Elswick Shipyard engineers, numbering between two and three hundred, were among those who received lockout notices.

Lord Armstrong's company was a leading member of the employers' federation, but sympathy for the workmen and their demand appears to have been widespread. On 20 July the *Newcastle Daily Journal* told its readers: 'In 1871, as now, the firm of Armstrong's was the centre of opposition. Then, as now, a federation of employers was formed for the purpose of resisting the demand, and then, as now, we were met with exactly the same arguments. Sir William (now Lord) Armstrong wrote to *The Times* stating a reduction from 59 to 54 hours per week would mean a loss to the employers of 17 per cent; that they had to suffer severe competition by both foreign makers and those at home; and that the men had fixed a hard and fast line which allowed of no negotiation whatever ... That the nine hours day has been entirely successful and that the evil prognostications of Lord Armstrong have been entirely falsified, is evidenced by the fact that his firm last year netted a clear profit amounting to £368,658, and yet these men, swollen with the pride of self, blinded by prejudice, conspire together, and to cajole other employers throughout the country to plunge an industry into confusion and bring misery into thousands of homes.'

Workers at the Elswick Shipyard in trades allied to the engineers were clearly hit by the dispute. On August 14 1897 the King of Siam stayed as an overnight guest at Cragside, Lord Armstrong's home in Northumberland. On the same day about 700 men received their notices at the shipyard. It was reported that 'the reason assigned for the necessity for giving notices is that owing to the backward state of the machinery required for certain war vessels it has been found necessary to reduce the shipyard staff.'

On 31 July 5,000 men demonstrated in favour of the eight-hour day at Newcastle's Haymarket. On 21 August a second demonstration was held, this time attended by at least 7,000 people. The workers assembled in Rye Hill and marched, complete with a band and banner, to the Haymarket. They were addressed by several speakers, including Keir Hardie, the pioneer of the Labour Movement whose efforts led to the foundation of the Labour Party. Hardie told the crowd that since the employers had on their own initiation forced the eight-hour issue to the front, the men would take them at their word and say: 'You have locked us out because you thought we wanted an eight-hours' day and now we shan't go in till we get it.'

AUGUST 23, 1897.

THE ENGINEERS' DISPUTE.

DEMONSTRATION IN NEWCASTLE HAYMARKET.

SPEECHES BY MR KEIR HARDIE AND MISS ENID STACEY.

From Newcastle Daily Journal.

He looked beyond the dispute to the time when the men would again be called upon, not to decide a lockout or a strike, but to decide whether the men who had locked them out should be allowed to continue to have a monopoly in the government of the country, or whether they as working men, with brains and votes, would also demand to have their representatives in the House of Commons. The interests to be decided at the ballot box were the same as those to be decided by that lockout.

Councillor J.C. Land told the meeting the position the workers were in had not been sought by them, but had been forced upon them. London would win in the struggle, he added, but the cockpit of the battle would be in Newcastle. By the arbitrary action they had taken the employers throughout the country had brought upon themselves the eight-hour day ten years sooner than it would otherwise have come. Mr T. Wilkinson, secretary of Newcastle, Gateshead and District Trades and Labour Council, put forward a motion: 'That this meeting condemns the action of the federated employers in locking out the workmen in the engineering trade, thus causing untold misery and suffering to thousands of innocent men, women and children, as well as unlimited damage to the commerce and industry of this country.' The motion was carried unanimously. Wilkinson urged every man present to join a trade union.

But cracks began to appear in the united front of the engineers. On 24 September a group of men returned to work at Elswick. The *Newcastle Daily Journal*, September 25, reported on the scenes at the Elswick Works that had taken place the day before. Several incidents of violent intimidation by strikers did occur during this phase of the dispute and there were a number of resulting prosecutions.

This national struggle was a great strain on the strike fund of the Amalgamated Engineers and by the end of October 1897 strike pay had to be reduced. The position of the engineers continued to deteriorate. On 18 January 1898 they were forced to withdraw their eight-hour day demand. The six-month battle was over. A ballot had been organised by the union to vote on a return to work, but J.W. Thwaites, secretary of Newcastle

EXCITEMENT AT ELSWICK.
ALLEGED INTIMIDATION.

Exciting scenes occurred yesterday near the Elswick Works, both during the dinner hour and at five o'clock when the men left work for the day. A crowd numbering some thousands assembled near the gates and several men were singled out for the unwelcome attention of the strikers, who were joined by a number of women and children. The men were followed to their respective homes, accompanied by much 'booing' and at times stronger expressions. Extra police were on duty and protected the men from violence.

*From **Newcastle Daily Journal**, 25 September, 1897.*

and Gateshead District of the union, was of the opinion that it did not matter much about the result of the vote because the financial position of the Amalgamated Engineers was so poor it was imperative for the men to return to work.

On 1 February the *Newcastle Daily Journal* informed its readers: 'Six hundred men began work at Armstrong, Whitworth and Co.'s, Elswick.' It added: 'All machinists and others will be engaged as the occasion arises. There is reported to be an abundance of work on hand and it is expected that before long all hands will be started.'

In 1871 the battling engineers had tasted the sweetness of victory. Now, in 1898, they experienced the bitterness of defeat.

Elswick Works, c. 1910

Colliers wait in mid-stream off Elswick to moor at Dunston Staithes around 1910. The Elswick Works and Shipyard are immediately behind them.

During the flourishing heyday of the Armstrong yard this stretch of the Tyne, twelve miles from the sea, was busy with shipping.

Chinese Sailors

Of the many warships built at the Elswick Yard, few could have aroused as much interest among the people of Newcastle as the Chinese cruisers *Chih Yuan* and *Ching Yuan*. The *Chih Yuan* was the first of the pair to be launched. The ceremony on 19 September 1886 was to Western onlookers an unusual affair. No women were allowed to be present and no brass band played the Chinese national anthem or a jaunty nautical air as she slid down the ways. Instead, cannons boomed in salute at the waterside.

Lord Sudeley, one of the dignitaries present, spoke about the ship's name when he addressed the reception following the launch. According to him *Chih Yuan* meant 'Go to far places and demolish all you come across'. His interpretation evoked a gale of laughter from some of the Western guests present. But Mr Fung Lee, who replied on behalf of the Chinese Minister in London, who was unable to be present, administered a polite diplomatic rebuke by remarking that 'there were perhaps not many who understood Chinese'. How correct he was. He went on to give his own translation of the cruiser's name: 'There is no distance to which this cruiser cannot extend and no enemies she is not able to overcome.' This time there was no laughter, only applause.

Early in June 1887 the Chinese transport ship, *Too Nan*, entered the Tyne and berthed alongside the grain warehouse on Newcastle's Quayside. Aboard her was Admiral W.M.

*The party assemble on the platform for the launch of the Chinese cruiser **Ching Yuan**. As with the **Chih Yuan**, no women were allowed to be present.*

*The Chinese cruiser **Chih Yuan,** launched at Elswick in 1886. She was sunk at the Battle of the Yalu during the Sino-Japanese War in 1894. The opposing ships at this engagement included the Elswick-built Japanese cruiser **Yoshino.***

Chinese hats, and dark blue suits with black velvet facings and trimmings. Members of a rank or grade described as 'secretaries' were resplendent in silken robes of light blue and white. Their every move seems to have been followed with great interest by the people of the city.

When Admiral Lang, accompanied by almost his entire force, attended a performance of a play at the Tyne Theatre and Opera House in Westgate Road they provided the other members of the audience with a talking point which may well have eclipsed the play. Nearly half of the pit had been reserved for the men. The officers were seated in the dress circle, while Admiral Lang and Captains Kew Pow Chin and Tan Shi Chang occupied a private box.

All 580 of them arrived after the performance had started. They marched up from the Quayside in columns of four. As each officer entered the theatre he presented his card. More than eighty crimson-coloured cards bearing Chinese characters with English translations were handed to the door keepers. An account in the *Newcastle Daily Journal* describes the scene inside the theatre: 'While the drop scene was down they were the cynosure of all European eyes. To English people, the sight of men-of-war men using fans seems very inappropriate but several of the officers, either

Lang and nearly 600 officers and men of the Imperial Chinese Navy. They had come to collect the two cruisers being built at Elswick and other warships nearing completion at Stettin in Prussia.

Newcastle had played host to seamen of many nationalities, but this sudden influx of Chinese sailors engendered more than the usual level of curiosity. Contemporary accounts describe the dress of the sailors: dark blue uniforms, light blue waist scarves and black turbans. The officers wore close fitting unaware of the effect they were making or indifferent to it, made use of their fans with all the ease, if not the grace, of a society lady.'

It seems that there were a few problems in the streets. A peppery letter to the press signed by 'M.M.' refers to the annoyance being caused to 'our visitors from China' by street boys who were 'not conspicuous for their display of good manners'. M.M. goes on to describe a particular incident. 'I was near the Central Station last night and one of the officers (who all the time seemed to be in the best of good humours) could scarcely get walked along for a lad stepping in front of him. I administered a sound box on the ears to the forward youth which caused him to desist; and I think if this were more generally done we would see less of these disgraceful scenes ...'

The burial of two Chinese sailors in St John's Cemetery, Elswick, caused the *Newcastle Daily Journal* to comment: '... the idle curiosity which in Newcastle follows all the walks abroad of the wanderers from the Flowery Land was not allowed to lapse even in the instance where death intervened.'

The sailors were Lien Chin Yuen, aged twenty-one, and Chin Shou-Fu, aged thirty, both natives of Foo Chien. They died in the Newcastle General Infirmary. At 4am on 6 June 1887 a contingent of forty of their shipmates, under the command of Captain Yeh, arrived at the Infirmary which was situated near where Marlborough Crescent is today. Carefully they wrapped the bodies in white sheets, then placed them in the coffins. Before the lids were secured the dead men's clothes were neatly folded up and laid beside them.

The gravestones of the three Chinese sailors who were buried in St John's Cemetery, Elswick, in 1887.

The Chinese coffins were very substantial affairs. They were black, built of strong wood, lined with lead and thickly coated with varnish. It took quite a long time and much effort to manhandle these five-hundredweight coffins from the mortuary on to the waiting hearses. The proceedings were watched by another sick Chinese man from one of the windows of the Infirmary 'doubtless with an interest of the most painful and mournful character'.

The cortège made its way up Westmorland Road. The hearses and the silent column of sailors then climbed Rye Hill and turned into Elswick Road. When the cemetery gates were reached an unexpected reception awaited them. About 200

The Elswick cruiser **Yoshino** *whose guns helped to sink the* **Chih Yuan.**

curious onlookers had got out of their beds at that early hour to witness the interment. They crowded closely around, determined not to miss a single aspect of the ceremony.

The graves had been dug close to those occupied by two Chinese sailors who had died of consumption aboard the transport ship *Hai Shin* while she lay at the Elswick Works in May 1881. After the coffins had been lowered into the graves the contingent of sailors, with their officers to the fore, knelt down in front of each grave in turn and silently bowed their heads to the earth five or six times. They then covered the coffins with soil and finished the funeral ceremony by igniting a heap of joss paper over each mound.

The nurses at the Infirmary paid their respects by sending a pair of wreaths, and two young sisters, the Misses Tailford, laid bouquets of flowers on the graves.

Six days later, again at 4am, another sailor, Chen Kin Quai, was laid to rest near his old comrades. Another large crowd had gathered and a police guard was mounted at the graveside. It was reported that on board the *Too Nan* nine other seamen were suffering from 'a malady peculiar to the Chinese'.

The gravestones of the three sailors still survive in St John's Cemetery, but they have been toppled over and now face downwards. Two Chinese headstones nearby, still in place, are those of the men from the transport ship *Hai Shin*.

An inscription fronting the headstones of the three men buried in 1887 read: 'The tombstones of these three and the two neighbouring graves were erected by the officers and crew of the Chinese cruisers *Chih Yuan* and *Ching Yuan*. To provide for these graves and the monument behind being kept in order a sum has been invested in the name of Mr Thos. Halliday who will apply the annual interest to that purpose.'

The *Too Nan* left the Tyne on 20 June 1887 with 291 of the sailors on board. They were on their way to Stettin to take delivery of two other cruisers. In August, it was the turn of the *Chih Yuan* and the *Ching Yuan* to depart the river. They steamed southwards to Spithead to rendezvous with the Stettin ships and a torpedo boat which had been built at Poplar.

At about this point, the ships began to be noticed as well as their colourful crews. Their fighting potential came as a shock to some observers. Commenting on the Elswick vessels a correspondent of the *Army and Navy Gazette* wrote: '... it is humiliating but nevertheless an actual fact that the two cruisers of the Chinese squadron are superior in certain novelties of construction to any of our own vessels. In point of speed they cannot be touched by our swiftest cruisers ...'

Within a few days all the newly-built ships had assembled in Spithead and before August was out they weighed anchor and sailed for China via Suez.

The *Chih Yuan* and the *Ching Yuan* served the Imperial Chinese Navy for less than ten years. Both were lost during the Sino-Japanese War of 1894-95. The *Ching Yuan* was sunk by shells fired from a fort at the Battle of Wei-Hai-Wei in February 1895. The *Chih Yuan* met her end at the Battle of the Yalu in September 1894 during a clash with a Japanese force which included the Elswick-built cruiser *Yoshino*. The *Chih Yuan* tried to ram the *Yoshino*, but failed to hit her faster opponent. The Chinese cruiser was then sunk by gunfire. It was ironic that the fortunes of war had pitted one Elswick ship against another.

Above, **the launch of the Chinese training cruiser** *Chao Ho* **on October 23 1911.**

This ship was probably the last to be launched abroad for Imperial China, shortly to be engulfed by revolution. The ceremony was performed by Miss Amy Lew, daughter of 'His Excellency, Yuk Lin Lew, Envoy Extraordinary and Minister Plenipotentiary to the Court of St James'. Unusually, the *Chao Ho* entered the Tyne with machinery and boilers on board, funnels fitted and other work in an advanced stage. After the ceremony, tea was served in the mould loft to representatives of the Chinese, Brazilian, Chilean, Spanish, Russian and Japanese navies as well as civic guests.

Below, **the front of the launch card issued to guests.**

LAUNCH OF THE
· CHINESE ·
TRAINING-CRUISER
"CHAO HO"
From the Elswick
Shipyard
Newcastle·on·Tyne.
by Miss AMY LEW

OCTOBER 23rd 1911

Battleship *Victoria*

HMS *Victoria* was the first battleship to be built at Elswick and at the time of her completion the heaviest and most expensive vessel ever constructed on the Tyne. She cost £724,855, a colossal sum by the standards of the 1880s.

Victoria's keel was laid on 13 June 1885, the same day as Elswick's first ship, the *Panther*, was launched. Guests who had assembled to see the *Panther* go down the ways were invited to witness Sir William Armstrong strike the first rivet into the structure of the new battleship. She was then known as the *Renown*, but only three weeks before her launch this was changed to *Victoria* in honour of Queen Victoria's Golden Jubilee Year, 1887.

The *Victoria*'s launch day, Saturday 9 April 1887, acquired all the trappings of a public holiday. Many local businesses closed. From early morning, spectators began arriving at every available vantage point on both sides of the river. About 3,500 tickets were issued for visitors to the shipyard alone. As Sir William had ceremoniously driven the first rivet into the ship, he was also on hand to strike home the last before the launch. By 3.30pm this task had been completed and the remaining chocks were knocked clear. Then, Mrs Forwood, wife of the Parliamentary Secretary to the Admiralty, pulled the handle of an apparatus which heaved a bottle of champagne against the *Victoria*'s bow. Right on cue, the great ship began to

*Sir William Armstrong (the top-hatted figure at the rear of the picture near the centre) surrounded by workers and spectators at the keel-laying ceremony of the battleship HMS **Victoria** in 1885.*

move, the band of the 3rd Volunteer Battalion of the Northumberland Fusiliers struck up *Rule Britannia* and a mighty cheer went up from the thousands of onlookers. As she entered the Tyne a huge wave was sent rolling across the river. It caught some of the less agile spectators standing on the opposite bank and gave them a thorough soaking.

After her launch the *Victoria* spent almost a year fitting out at Elswick. Her presence created an enormous amount of interest throughout Tyneside. In an unprecedented gesture, Armstrong Mitchell's allowed her to be inspected by the public on Easter Monday 1888. A sub-

*The launch of HMS **Victoria** on Saturday 9 April 1887.*
A huge wave was sent rolling across the Tyne, soaking some of the spectators on the Gateshead bank.

stantial charge of one shilling for morning visitors and two shillings for those who came in the afternoon did not prevent a big turnout of people eager to look over the largest ship most of them had ever seen.

At 10am on 6 April 1888 the *Victoria* left her moorings at Elswick to begin the journey down river to the sea. The spectacle attracted huge crowds. But for some who managed to get what should have been a choice viewing position on the High Level Bridge there was a disappointment in store. As the huge ship drew near, the *Daring*, one of the leading tugs, began

emitting voluminous clouds of dense black smoke. Added to this was a similar emission from the *Victoria*'s own two squat funnels. The battleship was completely enshrouded by the smoke.

Even in an era not exactly characterised by its environmental concern the incident brought unfavourable comment in the annual report of the Tyne Improvement Commissioners. It was suggested that an example should be made of the *Daring*. As for the *Victoria*, her smoke problem was so bad she had to have her funnels lengthened at an early stage in her career. Prior to that, life on her upper deck in anything but a beam wind must have been extremely uncomfortable.

The passage down river to the sea was accomplished in two stages. The first ended at the grain warehouse on the Quayside where she moored after being under way for only a couple of hours. She had negotiated the narrow south channel of the Swing Bridge without incident. The fact that a vessel with a breadth of 70ft and a draft of 26ft 9ins could safely navigate the Tyne above the Swing Bridge was an indication of how successful the Tyne Improvement Commission's work of recent years had been. Only twenty-five years before it had been possible to wade across the river at low water at the place where the High Level Bridge stands.

The *Victoria* got under way again the following morning, also at 10am. Soon after, she ran aground at Bill Quay. However, it was not long before the rising tide floated her off. As she passed the various shipyards the workmen were given time off to watch her go by. At North Shields boys of the training ship *Wellesley* manned the yards. It was here that HMS *Valorous* joined her. The *Valorous* was the last paddle frigate to be built for the Royal Navy. She was on hand to escort the *Victoria* to Chatham. After being swung for compass adjustment off Cullercoats and after a few preliminary engine trials, the *Victoria* departed for the southern naval base.

In 1890 the vessel became the flagship of the Commander in Chief of the Mediterranean Fleet, Vice Admiral Sir George Tryon. Fate was to bring disaster to both man and ship during fleet manoeuvres. In June 1893 the *Victoria* was leading one of two columns of ships, steaming along in parallel lines off Tripoli in North Africa. Admiral Tryon gave the order for the columns to reverse course by turning inwards towards one another. The order was obeyed. But the parallel lines of ships were not far enough apart to avoid calamity. Turning towards the *Victoria* and leading the other column was the battleship *Camperdown*. She struck the Elswick-built vessel a mortal blow on the starboard bow. Water rushed in and just over 10 minutes later the *Victoria* capsized. She then slid beneath the waves, taking with her 358 officers and men, including the admiral.

A court martial in Malta later that summer found that the loss of the *Victoria* was due to an order given by Vice Admiral Tryon. The ship's captain, Captain Maurice Bourke, was honourably acquitted of any blame. However, the court expressed its regret that Rear Admiral Hastings Markham, who was aboard the *Camperdown*, had not carried out his first intention of notifying the flagship that he doubted the possibility of completing the manoeuvre successfully.

Among the *Victoria*'s survivors was the then Lieutenant-Commander John Jellicoe who was to become Commander in Chief of the Grand Fleet at the Battle of Jutland during the First World War.

The news of the loss of the *Victoria* was read with shock on Tyneside, not least by the craftsmen of Elswick. There was a slight fear that their workmanship might have been in some way at fault, but reassurance on this point was soon forthcoming. The details are contained in an account by a correspondent of *The Globe* who interviewed the now Lord Armstrong at Cragside soon after the disaster. The correspondent wrote: 'While we sat talking, a servant came into the spacious living room bringing a letter. Lord Armstrong reads it, and, a slight smile of gratification passing over his venerable face, hands it to me. It is from Mr W.H. White, the Director of Naval Construction, and bore testimony to the fidelity and care with which, down to the smallest details, the *Victoria* was built at Elswick.'

Any sentiment or concern which the directors of Armstrong Mitchell had over the loss of the *Victoria* was put aside when it came to be measured in terms of hard cash. At a board meeting on 12 July 1893 the idea of contributing to the HMS *Victoria* Relief Fund was rejected.

Victoria **sails through the open Swing Bridge, Armstrong's gateway to the sea.**

The Swing Bridge between Newcastle and Gateshead was opened on July 17 1876. Thousands of spectators lined both sides of the river and crowded on to the High Level Bridge to see the first ship, the Italian Navy steamer *Europa* pass through on the north side of the central piers. The event took place 'amid cheers and the firing of cannon,' reported the *Newcastle Daily Journal*. Among those witnessing the opening were Sir William Armstrong and Captain Andrew Noble. The *Europa*, helped by two tugs, was on her way up river to Elswick to load a 100-ton gun built by Armstrong's for Italy. This was lifted aboard the next day by a 'ponderous hydraulic crane.'

Above, twelve years after the Swing Bridge first opened, the ill-fated battleship HMS *Victoria* passes through on 6 April 1888. Note the crowds on the High Level Bridge.

Warships for Japan

Three Japanese warships built at Elswick were sunk on the same day in 1904 during the Russo-Japanese War. The loss of these vessels marked one of the worst moments for Japan in the conflict at sea.

The first of the trio to be launched was the cruiser *Yoshino* (pictured on page 20). Named after a mountain noted for its cherry blossom, she slid down the ways on 12 December 1892. The launch ceremony was performed by the wife of Philip Watts, her designer. At the completion of steaming trials in July 1893, the *Yoshino* was heralded as 'the fastest cruiser in the world'. The results of these trials were undoubtedly impressive. Running against the tide she made over 22 knots and with the tide in her favour she exceeded 23. A Japanese crew was sent to Tyneside to man the *Yoshino* for the run home and on 30 September 1893 she was officially handed over.

A couple of days before the cruiser's departure she was lying off Jarrow Slake when news arrived that 2nd Cook Suyckichi Ouchi had died in the Infirmary. He had been involved in an accident at Elswick and developed pleurisy as a result. A funeral party from the ship travelled up the Tyne in their own steam launch to Elswick. A cortège was formed, the officers riding in cabs with the seamen following in procession on foot. A crowd of several hundred onlookers had assembled at St John's Cemetery and scenes reminiscent of the burial of the Chinese sailors six years previously were re-enacted.

The body of Suyckichi Ouchi was buried in a coffin which contained a new set of clothes and a pair of boots. A wooden monument with an inscription in Japanese was erected. After a wreath in a glass case had been placed over the grave, the seaman's last resting place was sprinkled with water. Then the officers, followed by the men, stepped one by one to the foot of the grave and bowed.

The second to be launched, of the three ships sunk in 1904, was the *Yashima*. She was the first battleship built for the Imperial Japanese Navy at Elswick. Her keel was laid down on 6 December 1894 and she took twenty months to complete. Bearing the ancient poetic name of Japan, the *Yashima* was one of the largest and most formidable warships of her day. The ship's main armament consisted of four 12-inch guns and the secondary armament included twenty three-pounder guns. There were five torpedo tubes. Her armoured belt was eighteen inches thick over the machinery spaces. The launch of the *Yashima* was scheduled for 2.30pm on 28 February 1896, but when the time arrived the tide was not high enough. A strong westerly wind blowing down the Tyne was blamed for keeping the water back. It took another thirty minutes before the tide reached its predicted height. When it did, Madam Kato, wife of the Japanese Minister in London, released a bottle of champagne which smashed against the ship's bow. As it did so a flock of pigeons was released and after a moment's hesitation the *Yashima* slid gracefully into the Tyne.

Following the ceremony, lunch was provided in the dining room of the Ordnance Works for a number of the most distinguished guests. Lord Armstrong, Earl and Lady Percy and Captain Yendo, the Japanese Naval Attaché, were among those present. Sir Andrew Noble proposed a toast: 'To the designer of the *Yashima* – Mr Philip Watts.' On 14 May 1897, shortly before her completion, the battleship was moored at Newcastle's Quayside and thrown open to the public for viewing. Excursion trains were run from as far away as Berwick and Carlisle. Proceeds went to the New Infirmary Fund.

The third vessel was the battleship *Hatsuse*, launched on 27 June 1899. At that date she was the largest warship ever to come from the Tyne's slipways. On the same day, another

*The Japanese battleship **Yashima** off Newcastle Quayside, where the vessel was moored for public viewing.*
She hit at least one mine at Port Arthur in 1904, but remained afloat for several hours before sinking. This enabled most of her crew to be rescued.

record-breaking vessel was launched by Armstrong Whitworth, the merchant ship *Atlantian*. Built at the company's Walker yard, she was the river's largest merchant vessel at that date. A contemporary account describes her as 'a peaceful argosy capable of transporting 11,500 tons'.

Such a description could hardly be applied to the *Hatsuse*, which, like the *Yashima*, carried four 12-inch guns. It was 5.30pm when the last chocks were knocked from beneath the *Hatsuse*. Her launching weight was 8,500 tons. The spectacle of such a large ship entering the water naturally attracted many sightseers. From Newcastle Quayside came the Tyne General Ferry Company's steamer *Syren*, crowded from stem to stern.

Madam Arakawa, wife of the Japanese Consul General in London, performed the launching ceremony. She was watched by the Japanese Chargé d'Affaires and representatives of the navies of the United States, Norway, Portugal, Chile and of course Japan. All these nations had ships in various stages of construction at Elswick.

The completion of the *Hatsuse* in January 1901 coincided with the death of Queen Victoria. One of the new battleship's first duties after leaving the Tyne was to steam to Spithead to join the warships of many nations lining the route from East Cowes to Portsmouth taken by the Royal Yacht *Alberta* as she bore the Queen's body from the Isle of Wight to the mainland. When the maritime cortège steamed by, the crews of the ships stood to attention on deck with heads bowed. Ensigns were dipped as a further mark of respect.

The Russo-Japanese War opened on the night of 8 February 1904 with an attack by Japanese destroyers against ships of the Russian Pacific Fleet lying at anchor off Port Arthur. The *Hatsuse* became the flagship of Rear Admiral Nashiba who was in command of the warships blockading the Russian-controlled port in north-eastern China. Among the vessels also taking part in the blockade were the *Yashima* and *Yoshino*. On 9 February, when the first shots were exchanged with the shore batteries, a shell exploded in the admiral's cabin, killing or wounding sixteen men. It was a bad start, but worse was to come.

In April the Japanese sank the battleship *Petropavlovsk*.

Among those killed was the brilliant Russian officer Admiral Makarov who was aboard her. The sinking had been achieved by sowing mines at the entrance to Port Arthur. It was a lesson not lost on the Russians. Captain Ivanoff, commander of the minelayer *Amur*, spotted a weakness in the operations of the blockading Japanese ships – they never varied their patrol lines. This predictability was to prove disastrous. On 14 May the *Amur* slipped out of harbour, evading the enemy, and laid mines across the patrol lines. The following morning along came the patrolling *Hatsuse*, *Yashima* and *Shikishima*.

The *Hatsuse* was the first to hit one of the mines. The explosion which followed wrecked her steering gear and she became unmanageable. A towline from another vessel was put aboard but soon afterwards she struck a second mine. A series of explosions followed. Within a few minutes the *Hatsuse* sank, taking more than 500 officers and men with her.

Next, it was the *Yashima*'s turn. It was thought she might have struck two mines. Whatever the number, she was holed badly. For a while her watertight bulkheads stayed intact and she remained afloat. A determined effort was made to tow the *Yashima* to safety but failed. After several hours she capsized. Fortunately, her crew had ample time to abandon ship and loss of life was small. On the same day the cruiser *Yoshino* was manoeuvring in dense fog to the south of the Liao-Tung Peninsula on which Port Arthur is situated. Suddenly the Japanese armoured cruiser *Kasuga* loomed out of the murk and struck the *Yoshino* a fatal blow. A large hole was torn in her port quarter and she began to sink rapidly by the stern. This time, loss of life was heavy – numbers reported vary between 318 and 329 officers and men. But the Japanese were to eventually win their war with Russia. At the Battle of Tsushima on 27-28 May 1905 Admiral Togo's ships inflicted total defeat upon the Russian Baltic Fleet commanded by Admiral Zinovi Rojestvensky. On the Russian side, 4,830 men were killed and eight battleships, four cruisers and five destroyers sunk. Nearly all their other ships were captured, wrecked or interned in neutral ports. Only three vessels managed to escape to the safety of Vladivostok. In contrast, the Japanese lost 117 men and only three torpedo boats. Togo's victory had been overwhelming.

*Three cheers! Hats are raised as the Japanese battleship **Hatsuse** glides down the ways on 27 June 1899.*

*A fine view of the Japanese armoured cruiser **Asama** leaving the Tyne assisted by a paddle tug. Launched in 1898, she was damaged at the Battle of Tsushima in 1905 but managed to rejoin the fray. The **Asama** survived the Second World War, being broken up in 1946-47.*

The *Iwate* is born.

The Japanese cruiser *Iwate* after her launch at Elswick on 30 March 1900. At the Battle of Tsushima she was hit sixteen times but sustained only minor damage. During mopping-up operations on the second day of the battle she played a leading role in sinking the Russian battleship *Admiral Ushakoff*. The Russian vessel fought bravely for three hours against the *Iwate* and another cruiser, the *Yakumo*. Hit below the waterline, the battleship eventually turned over and went down with the loss of eighty-two officers and men. Later in her career the *Iwate* became a training ship and survived until the Second World War. In July 1945 US carrier-borne aircraft located her near Kure, Japan, and she was attacked, sinking in shallow water.

The gathering for the launch of the battleship *Kashima*.

The lady with the bouquet (third from left on platform) is Madam Arakawa, wife of the Japanese Consul General in London, who performed the ceremony. On the extreme left of the platform is Lady Noble, wife of company chairman Sir Andrew Noble. Suspended high above them from the ship's bows is a decorated cage containing pigeons to be released. Madam Arakawa was by this time a well known lady at Elswick. She had also launched the *Asama*, *Iwate* and *Hatsuse*. It was a bright, sunny day when the *Kashima* slid down the ways on 22 March 1905. The *Newcastle Daily Journal* described the scene: 'She was much admired as she lay on the stocks, gaily decorated with Japanese flags, evergreens etc. Suspended from her bow was a large collapsible cage covered with red and white striped material and containing a number of pigeons, which in accordance with national custom were released, together with a quantity of confetti, as the vessel glided into the water amid enthusiastic cheering from the crowds. The birds at once took flight, which, it may be observed, was regarded as a good omen. Had they alighted on the ship, the latter, if there be anything in superstition, would be doomed to an unlucky career.'

Togo's Heroes at St James' Park, April 1906.

In April 1906 Japanese sailors arrived on Tyneside to take delivery of the battleship *Kashima* which had been launched at Elswick the previous year. The *Kashima* was the last warship to be built at the yard for the Imperial Japanese Navy. It was the end of an era, for it was no longer necessary for Japan to have such vessels built abroad. The Land of the Rising Sun was now able to construct its own warships. More than 100 men of the *Kashima* and a group of officers watched a football match at St James' Park between Newcastle and Stoke during their visit to the city. The crew had spent the afternoon of Tuesday 24 April 1906 looking around the city centre. When they arrived at the football ground they found welcoming messages displayed in Japanese writing. The men had tea with club directors and received a cheer from the crowd as they took their places on the stand. The crowd cheered again when the officers stood to attention during the playing of their country's national anthem. Many of the sailors had fought at the Battle of Tsushima in 1905 and were regarded as heroes. The *Newcastle Weekly Chronicle* reported: 'The game excited the men's liveliest attention, and good play was applauded generously.' Newcastle scored a resounding 5 – 0 victory in front of a 12,000 crowd.

*The launch cards (slightly smaller than actual size) for the United States cruiser **Albany**.*

Launch cards were issued to official guests at launching ceremonies. They were intended to be colourful and informative souvenirs. The cards carried an attractive artist's impression of the ship in service, the flag of her country and the vessel's particulars, such as her tonnage and dimensions.

Here the United States cruiser *Albany* is depicted on a launch card entering New York harbour. She was named after the capital of New York State. Originally ordered from Elswick in 1897 by the Brazilian government, she was bought by the US Navy in March 1898 when war between America and Spain became imminent. The ship was still on the stocks when purchased and was not launched until January the following year, by which time the Spanish-American War had ended. During the First World War the *Albany* acted as a convoy escort in the Atlantic.

Another American cruiser was also built at Elswick, the *New Orleans*. She was launched two years before the *Albany* and was also purchased from Brazil. Originally named *Amazonas*, the ship was handed over to the Americans shortly after completion in March 1898. The *New Orleans* took part in the blockade of Cuba and Puerto Rico during the Spanish-American War.

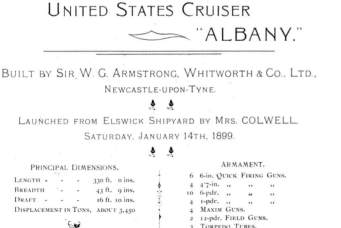

UNITED STATES CRUISER
"ALBANY."

BUILT BY SIR W. G. ARMSTRONG, WHITWORTH & CO., LTD.,
NEWCASTLE-UPON-TYNE.

LAUNCHED FROM ELSWICK SHIPYARD BY MRS. COLWELL.
SATURDAY, JANUARY 14TH, 1899.

PRINCIPAL DIMENSIONS.	ARMAMENT.
LENGTH - - - 330 ft. 0 ins.	6 6-in. QUICK FIRING GUNS.
BREADTH - - 43 ft. 9 ins.	4 4·7-in. ,, ,, ,,
DRAFT - - - 16 ft. 10 ins.	10 6-pdr. ,, ,, ,,
DISPLACEMENT IN TONS, ABOUT 3,450	4 1-pdr. ,, ,, ,,
	4 MAXIM GUNS.
	2 12-pdr. FIELD GUNS.
	3 TORPEDO TUBES.

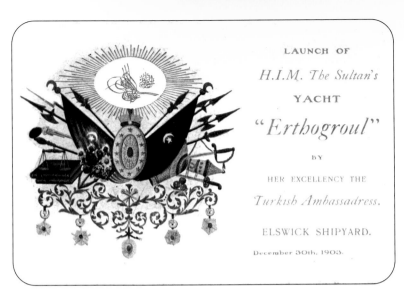

The cards pictured on this page were produced for the steam yacht *Erthogroul*, launched for the Sultan of Turkey in 1903.

Internal fittings and decorations were by Waring and Sons (later Waring and Gillow Ltd.) who had also been responsible for the interiors in the British and German royal yachts, the *Victoria and Albert* and *Hohenzollern* respectively. The Turkish Imperial saloon was framed and panelled in mahogany and gold. The furniture and a piano matched the panelling. Seats were upholstered in silk.

Erthogroul was launched by the wife of the Turkish ambassador, Masurus Pacha. Among those present at the ceremony was the ship's designer, J.R. Perrett.

The engines were supplied by Hawthorn Leslie's St Peter's Works and gave her a speed of 18 knots. She carried eight quick-firing guns. As late as 1959 the vessel was reported to be still afloat but partly dismantled.

*The launch cards for the Turkish steam yacht **Erthogroul**.*

H. I M. THE SULTAN'S . .

TWIN-SCREW STEAM YACHT

"ERTHOGROUL,"

BUILT BY

Sir W. G. ARMSTRONG, WHITWORTH & Co., Limited,
Newcastle-on-Tyne.

Principal Dimensions:

	Ft.	Ins.		Ft.	In.
Length (BETWEEN PERPENDICULARS) .	260	0	Depth, Moulded	15	0
Breadth, Moulded . . .	27	6	Draft, Mean :	10	0

Displacement: 900 Tons.

Armament:

8 3-Pdr. Quick-Firing Guns.

The Disappearance of HMS *Wasp*

A delicately sculptured fountain is situated above the old harbour at Cullercoats. It is dedicated to the memory of a local man and his Elswick-built ship, Lieutenant Commander Bryan John Huthwaite Adamson, captain of the gunboat HMS *Wasp*.

Cullercoats born and bred, Lieutenant Commander Adamson was in his mid-thirties when appointed to the newly-built *Wasp*. She was his first, only and last command. In a naval career dating back to 1866 when he left the Britannia Naval College he had served in many parts of the world. His entire career had been spent aboard ships of the transitional period between sail and steam. All of them had engines and most carried a good spread of canvas and were capable of sustained ocean passages under sail alone. This was often done when winds were favourable to conserve their coal bunkers. Managing a ship with the barquentine sailing rig of the *Wasp* as well as an engine would have presented few problems to him.

HMS *Wasp* was launched at Elswick on 13 September 1886. The number thirteen has some superstitious associations among seafarers. So should the name *Wasp*. Just why the Admiralty had chosen such a name for the newly-built gunboat is a mystery. Only two years before the launch another gunboat bearing the name *Wasp* had struck an isolated rock off the west coast of Ireland and gone down with fifty-two of her crew, including the captain. Only six had been saved. The details of this disaster must have been fresh in the minds of many seafaring men as the new *Wasp* slid down the ways into the Tyne.

She left the river on 30 December 1886. In April the following year the *Wasp* was commissioned for service in Chinese waters and on 21 May set out on the long passage towards Shanghai. The gunboat's route took her through the Mediterranean and the Suez Canal, then down the Red Sea from where her crew, in letters home, complained of the very hot weather. Then it was across the Indian Ocean to Singapore which was to be her last stop before heading northwards

The drinking fountain in Cullercoats erected in memory of Lieutenant Commander Bryan John Huthwaite Adamson, c. 1920s.

*The **Rattler** and **Wasp** on the stocks at Elswick. The **Wasp** is on the right, in an earlier stage of construction than her sister.*

towards her final destination. By the time Singapore was reached, the satisfaction and novelty of a first command had soured for Lieutenant Commander Adamson. His feelings were expressed in a letter written to his mother: 'I don't care much for my command; things may turn out better but with the two inexperienced officers I have to assist me I am captain, first lieutenant and navigator all in one. Since leaving England I have never been in bed before daylight at sea.'

Crew member John Roach, a carpenter, made an even more serious allegation about his immediate superior in a letter to his father. He stated that the mate he was under had never been aboard a ship before and was altogether incompetent for the job. John Roach went on to say that the *Wasp* was undermanned and the seamen terribly hard-worked.

The problem of undermanning had also troubled Adamson. While the *Wasp* was at Sheerness he had petitioned his superiors for twelve additional able seamen. Only eight had been allocated. The situation was aggravated still further on the passage out. An accident aloft had robbed him of a crew member he described as his 'smartest seaman'. This man had to be landed in Ceylon. He was lucky.

It cannot have been a very happy ship which stood out from Singapore on 10 September 1887. There were eighty souls on board. Seventy-three of these made up the *Wasp*'s regular complement. The rest were men on their way to join other ships on the China Station. They expected to reach Shanghai around 21 September but never did. For they and the *Wasp* simply disappeared without trace.

It was thought that she foundered while traversing the South China Sea during a typhoon which was known to have been raging at the time. Other shipping certainly suffered. On 15 September the Chinese transport vessel *Waylee* was driven ashore on the Pescadores with the loss of 285 lives. Five days later the British barque *Oxford* came to grief on the coast of Bataan in the Philippines and the steamship *Anton* had her decks swept by an enormous sea which carried overboard the second mate and twenty-four Chinese.

As the days passed and no tidings of the *Wasp* came to hand the anxious naval authorities at Hong Kong sent warships fanning out into the South China Sea to look for her. The cruiser *Leander* and the gunboat *Cockchafer* went to the Paracel Islands. HMS *Firebrand*, a tiny 450-ton gunboat, concentrated on Pratas Shoal. From Singapore the cable steamer *Recorder* combed the islands to the north of that place as well as the coast of Cochin China and Hainan Island. Another ship which became involved in the search was the screw corvette HMS *Calliope*. In later years the *Calliope* was moored at Elswick as the training ship of the Tyne Division of the Royal Naval Volunteer Reserve. Like all the others, she found nothing.

The search continued throughout October and into November. A report in the *Newcastle Daily Journal* of 2 November 1887 stated that the *Wasp*'s sister ship, the Elswick-built HMS *Rattler*, had been sent to search the Cocos Islands and that other vessels from Singapore were 'making enquiries'. Finally, at the beginning of December the Admiralty published the following notice: 'All hopes for the safety of HMS *Wasp* having now been relinquished, directions have been given that her books are to be considered closed on the 6th December 1887, and the balance of the wages due up to that date is to be paid to the representatives of the officers and men.'

A few days later, Dr Frank Rennie, a close friend of Lieutenant Commander Adamson, proposed that a memorial drinking fountain be erected in Cullercoats where Lieutenant Commander Adamson 'was so well known and beloved'.

Dick Keys

Loss of the *Cobra*

Cobra undergoing sea-trials, c. 1900-1901.

The invention of the marine steam turbine engine by Sir Charles Parsons was to revolutionise the propulsion of warships and passenger liners. In 1897 Parsons had cleverly demonstrated the capabilities of his turbine engine by staging a display of speed at Queen Victoria's Diamond Jubilee Fleet Review. His long, sleek steam yacht *Turbinia* had raced past the warships assembled in Spithead at a speed of over 34 knots.

However, even before this display Armstrong Whitworth had been interested in the idea of fitting the turbine engine in one of its vessels. The company made the decision to install the machinery in a torpedo boat destroyer which would be built 'on spec' in the hope of finding a buyer. HMS *Cobra*, as the ship was to become, was launched at Elswick on 28 June 1899.

Her structural arrangements were based on those of two other vessels built at Elswick for the Admiralty in 1895. However, there was one major difference. The turbine machinery of the *Cobra* weighed 183 tons. That was 73 tons more than the machinery in the other two ships and 30 tons heavier than had been envisaged. But designer Philip Watts was later to state that 'a margin for such an eventuality had been incorporated in the original design'.

The *Cobra* was offered for sale to the Admiralty in December 1899. However, the naval authorities were unhappy with certain aspects of the ship and demanded that modifications be made before they would accept her. The main requirement was that her upper deck be strengthened. This was duly carried out.

The *Cobra* had been launched two months before HMS *Viper*, another turbine-driven torpedo boat destroyer which was built by Hawthorn Leslie of Hebburn. But the *Viper* was completed ahead of the *Cobra* and became the world's first turbine-driven warship. This distinction would have gone to the *Cobra* had it not been for a collier running into her as she lay alongside her fitting-out quay at Elswick. The damage took seven months to repair.

On 8 May 1900 the *Cobra* was sold to the Admiralty for £63,500. In June she clocked up a speed of 34.89 knots on trials. It was not until September the following year that the ship was ready to leave her builders. There were seventy-nine men aboard her for the run from the Tyne to Portsmouth where she was to be armed and commissioned. Twenty-four were from the North-East – mainly employees of Armstrong Whitworth and of Parsons, the turbine builders. Included among them were two distinguished engineers, Magnus Sandison and Robert Barnard. Sandison had been superintendent engineer at Elswick since the yard was first opened. He was the designer of a special type of marine engine known as the 'six-crank'. Robert Barnard was the manager of the Parsons company which was based on the Tyne. He had assisted in the design of the *Turbinia* and had supervised her construction. He had also been closely involved with the building of the *Cobra*, *Viper* and *King Edward*, the first turbine-driven passenger vessel.

At 5pm on 9 September 1901 the *Cobra* sailed from the Tyne. To begin with all went well and she ran along at 17 knots. But as the night wore on the weather began to deteriorate. The new torpedo boat destroyer started to roll so heavily that it was impossible for the men to work in her cramped stoke-hold. Speed had to be reduced to four or five knots. When daylight came it was possible to increase speed slightly.

At 7am a lightship was sighted on the starboard bow. Sandison made his way forward to try to identify it. Suddenly there was a distinct shock as if the ship had 'gone over something'. Within seconds the *Cobra* had broken in two.

The crew of the Outer Dowsing Light Vessel off the

Magnus Sandison, photographed the day before the ***Cobra*** *sailed from the Tyne.*

Lincolnshire coast had watched with interest as the *Cobra* came into view. Their interest turned to horror as she suddenly seemed to blow up in a cloud of steam and smoke. They thought she was the victim of a boiler explosion. Immediately danger signals were hoisted aboard the lightship. Four guns were fired in an effort to attract the attention of a passing steamer, but she held her course until out of sight, oblivious to the disaster she was leaving behind.

At 4.30pm Yarmouth Herring Boat No. 15 was drifting for fish near the Outer Dowsing Buoy. As she went along with the tide No. 15 found herself amongst a group of bodies all wearing lifebelts which 'had proved to be death traps; some of the men were floating with their feet uppermost'. The bodies of four sailors and two civilians were hauled aboard the fishing boat. Her skipper, John Smith, made for Grimsby to report the disaster. On the way, he spoke to the lightship men. By this time more bodies were floating past the anchored vessel.

At 6pm the P & O steamer *Harlington* was heading north on passage from London to Middlesbrough under the command of a Captain Young. He was chatting to his chief engineer, Mr James of Newcastle, when they sighted a small boat a couple of miles to the south of them. Course was altered to investigate. The boat proved to be the *Cobra*'s 14ft dinghy with twelve men on board. They were the only survivors. Sandison and Barnard were not among them.

A court martial to try the surviving crew and inquire into the loss of the *Cobra* was convened aboard HMS *Victory* at Portsmouth on 10 October 1901. Much of the evidence centred around the construction of the vessel. Philip Watts told the court a number of sea trials had been made in bad weather and the *Cobra* had come through these in a most satisfactory manner. Naval construction officials spoke well of her.

The mate in charge of the Outer Dowsing Light Vessel, Samuel Hambling, faced an awkward question at the hearing. The lightship was equipped with two boats, one 20ft and one 14ft long. He had a crew of six, all experienced boatmen. Hambling told the court there was too much wind and sea to launch a boat. This brought the question from the court: 'You say that there was too much wind and sea for you to use your boat. How do you account for the fact that a 14ft boat of the *Cobra* with twelve men on board succeeded in remaining in it for eleven hours?'

Hambling quoted his instructions which forbade him from leaving the lightship on any pretext. The matter does not seem to have been pursued any further, but his decision not to put out a boat may well have troubled his conscience for the rest of his life.

The findings of the court martial were announced on 16 October 1901. They were not complimentary to Armstrong Whitworth. It was found that the *Cobra* did not touch the seabed or meet any obstruction; nor was her loss due to any error of navigation but was attributable to the 'weakness' of the ship. The court also found that the *Cobra* was weaker than other destroyers, and it was 'to be regretted that she was purchased into His Majesty's Service'.

No blame was attached to any of the survivors and they were fully acquitted. Torpedo-Coxswain Francis Barnes was praised for the way in which he had handled the dinghy and the survivors on board.

An informed journal, *The Mariner*, tried to put the disaster

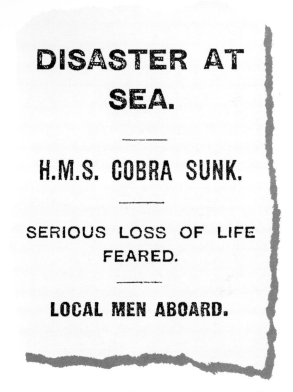

DISASTER AT SEA.

—

H.M.S. COBRA SUNK.

—

SERIOUS LOSS OF LIFE FEARED.

—

LOCAL MEN ABOARD.

*From **Newcastle Daily Chronicle**, 20 September 1901 .*

into perspective in an article later that year: '… the findings of the court would be a terrible indictment on the reputation of the great Elswick firm, the designers and builders of the *Cobra*, did it not admit of very considerable qualification. Those who are conversant with such matters know full well that the Armstrong firm bears a world wide reputation no less on account of the high scientific attainments of its staff than for the completeness of its equipment and the skill of its employees.'

Sixty-seven men had lost their lives in the disaster. Many of them were from Tyneside. A fund was set up to help their dependents. Armstrong Whitworth contributed £1,000.

Fate was no kinder to the *Cobra*'s sister, HMS *Viper*. This vessel also had a short-lived career. She was wrecked on rocks near Alderney in the Channel Islands in August 1901.

Beri-Beri

Ships are usually remembered for such factors as tragedy, novelty, fighting reputation, luxury, speed or good looks. However, the Elswick-built cruiser *Barroso* should perhaps be remembered for a disease – beri-beri.

Built for the Brazilian Navy, the ship was launched on 25 August 1896 by Madam Sisson, wife of Commander Sisson, secretary of the Brazilian Naval Commission in Europe. 'The ceremony was performed under the most happy and auspicious circumstance,' reported the *Newcastle Daily Journal*. 'The weather was delightfully fine and in consequence a very large number of ladies and gentlemen were present, the former being costumed in the brightest and most picturesque of summer garbs.'

The *Barroso*, or *Almirante Barroso* as she is sometimes referred to, carried six 6-inch guns and four 4.7-inch quick-firing guns. Driven by triple expansion engines, she was capable of 20.5 knots.

Nowadays, beri-beri is usually only met with in countries of the world where the staple diet is polished rice, but until relatively recent years it was frequently met with at sea. Indeed, it was as much a seamen's disease as the more publicised scurvy, and like that condition it is also caused by a vitamin deficiency. The disease occurs in two forms. There is the dry type, which gives rise to paralysis and severe pains in the arms and legs, and the wet type, which is characterised by marked oedema and heart failure. Dry or wet, both are serious conditions.

For part of her career the *Barroso* was bedeviled by this scourge. It first occurred amongst her crew in 1904. Four years later there was another outbreak. At the time beri-beri was reported to be prevalent in North Brazil, the *Barroso*'s home territory.

On 3 July 1909 she left Rio de Janeiro with a crew of 434 on board. A call was made at Recife. Then she steamed across the South Atlantic to St Vincent in the Cape Verde Islands, where she stayed for a short period before heading northwards to Las Palmas in the Canary Islands. Forty days after leaving Rio she put into Plymouth. While there two seamen complained of an illness which the ship's surgeon diagnosed as beri-beri. From Plymouth the *Barroso* continued her northward journey towards the Tyne, probably in connection with the commissioning of the two scout cruisers *Bahia* and *Rio Grande do Sul* being built at Elswick.

While in the river three more of her crew went down with the illness. Dr W.E. Harker, the Medical Officer of Health on the Tyne, had these men taken to the floating hospital at Jarrow Slake. Soon they were joined by more of their shipmates until no fewer than forty had been admitted to the same hospital. It is interesting to note the treatment received by these men. To begin with rice was eliminated from their diet. Ample quantities of fresh vegetables, fruit and milk were given. Additional measures were also taken. 'Suspecting that the toxin might gain entrance by the alimentary tract,' wrote Dr Harker, 'I have given an intestinal disinfectant followed in the morning by a mild aperient of sulphur of soda. As a general tonic quinine with strychnine in small doses appears to do good.'

In the light of more modern knowledge it is probable that the change of diet did more good than Dr Harker's additional treatment, but the fact remains that there was only one fatality. None of the officers were affected. At the time this was largely accounted for by their better standard of accommodation, but the more varied diet available to them would have been nearer the truth.

Beri-beri was not confined to foreign vessels. Four years

*The cruiser **Barroso**, launched for the Brazilian Navy in 1896. Crew members were affected by the disease beri-beri.*

after the *Barroso*'s visit to the Tyne, a North Shields-owned bar-quentine, the *Sound of Jura*, was towed into the Cape Verde Islands by the Newcastle tramp steamer *Uskmoor* after being found near derelict in the South Atlantic with most of her crew incapacitated by the disease.

The *Barroso*, like most Elswick ships of the 1890s, was designed by Philip Watts, who was knighted in 1905. Sir Philip

had succeeded Sir William White as naval architect and general manager at the yard in 1885. Sir William left Tyneside to become Admiralty director of naval construction. Sir Philip followed in his predecessor's footsteps for a second time when in 1902 he took over the same post at the Admiralty.

Leading Elswick naval architects after 1902 included J.R. Perrett and Sir Eustace H. Tennyson D'Eyncourt.

Defender of Norway.

An imposing view of the Norwegian coast defence battleship *Norge* on trials in the North Sea. Launched in March 1900, the *Norge* had a long and peaceful career until the invasion of her country by German forces during the Second World War. She was sunk by torpedoes fired from a German destroyer at Narvik in April 1940. Out of a crew of 199 officers and men there were eighty-nine survivors. The ship managed to engage the destroyer in a short gun duel before meeting her end. On the same day, her sister, the Elswick-built *Eidsvold*, also launched in 1900, blew up and sank as a result of a German torpedo attack outside Narvik harbour. Only eight of her ninety-three-man crew survived.

World War I and After

With the outbreak of the First World War in 1914 Elswick warships were called upon to play their role in the unfolding conflict. Among them was the battlecruiser HMS *Invincible* which, with her sister *Inflexible*, defeated a German squadron at the Battle of the Falklands in 1914. However, later in the war the *Invincible* was to meet tragedy. She was sunk at the Battle of Jutland in 1916 with the loss of 1,020 lives.

Other Elswick vessels at Jutland were the battleships *Agincourt*, *Canada*, *Superb* and *Monarch* and the cruisers *Hampshire* and *Birmingham*. All these survived that immense clash of fleets in the North Sea. But less than a week afterwards the *Hampshire* was sunk when she struck a mine while taking Lord Kitchener to Russia. Kitchener went down with the cruiser.

The final warship built at the Elswick Yard was the aircraft carrier HMS *Eagle*. Originally laid down as a battleship for Chile, work on her was halted between 1914 and 1917. Afterwards, she was bought by Britain and converted into an aircraft carrier. The vessel was launched in 1918.

Running trials in 1920, the *Eagle* was eventually completed in 1924. She left the Tyne as the first carrier to have a superstructure situated on the extreme starboard side of the ship. This became a standard design feature.

The departure of the *Eagle* marked the end of an era at Elswick. The yard closed and all shipbuilding was switched to the Walker Naval Yard further down river which had opened in 1913.

The *Eagle* went on to give stirling service to the Royal Navy in the Mediterranean. However, she was lost in August 1942 when torpedoed and sunk by a U-boat between Algiers and Majorca. The majority of servicemen on board were rescued.

HMS **Eagle,** *an early aircraft carrier, launched in 1918, torpedoed in 1942.*

Today, there is barely any trace of the once great Elswick Shipyard. Its site is occupied by part of a business park. Modern offices and neatly laid out roads are named after warships built there, such as Panther House, Asama Court and Monarch Road. A pleasant walkway along the banks of the Tyne passes over the spot where giant vessels of steel attracted huge crowds as they were launched into a flourishing river so many years ago.

Vessels launched from the Elswick Shipyard

Abbreviations: r/n = Re-named. b/u = Broken up.

WARSHIPS

1885 *Panther*, Austro-Hungarian cruiser. c.1920: b/u.

1885 *Salamina*, Greek cruiser. 1887: Sold to Italy, r/n *Angelo Emo*, then *Dogali* before completion. 1908: Sold to Uruguay, r/n *24 de Agosto*, later *Montevideo*. 1912: Reported wrecked on coast of Brazil but remained listed until 1931.

1885 *Leopard*, Austro-Hungarian cruiser. 1931: b/u.

1885 *Chih Yuan*, Chinese cruiser. 1894: Sunk in action with Japanese.

1886 *Rattler*, British gunboat. 1919: r/n *Dryad*. 1924: b/u.

1886 *Wasp*, British gunboat. 1887: Disappeared on passage Singapore to Shanghai.

1886 *Isla de Luzon*, Spanish cruiser. 1898: Captured by U.S. during Spanish American War. 1923: Sold for use as salvage vessel, r/n *Reviver*. c.1924: b/u.

1886 *Ching Yuan*, Chinese cruiser. 1895: Sunk in action with Japanese. 1895/6: Raised and scrapped.

1887 *Isla de Cuba*, Spanish cruiser. 1898: Captured by U.S. during Spanish-American War. 1912: Transferred to Venezuela, r/n *Mariscal Sucre*. 1940: b/u.

1887 *Elizabeta*, Rumanian cruiser. 1929: Used as barrack hulk for boys at Constanza.

1887 *Victoria*, British battleship. Laid down as *Renown*. 1893: Sank following collision.

1888 *Piemonte*, Italian cruiser. c.1920: Deleted.

1889 *Wizard*, Australian torpedo gunboat.1890: r/n *Karrakatta*. 1905: b/u.

1889 *Whiting*, Australian torpedo gunboat. 1890: r/n *Boomerang*. 1905: b/u.

1889 *Pelorus*, Australian cruiser. 1890: r/n *Mildura*. 1906: b/u.

1889 *Pandora*, Australian cruiser. 1890: r/n *Katoomba*.1906: b/u.

1890 *Necochea*, Argentine cruiser, r/n *25 de Mayo* before completion. c.1916: b/u.

1890 *Sirius*, British cruiser, 1918: Sunk as block ship at Ostend.

1890 *Persian*, Australian cruiser. 1890: r/n *Wallaroo*. 1919: r/n *Wallington*. 1920: r/n *Wallaroo*, then b/u.

1890 *Plassy*, Royal India Marine torpedo gun boat. 1904: b/u.

1891 *Spartan*, British cruiser. 1921: r/n *Defiance II*. 1931: b/u.

1891 *Assaye*, Royal India Marine torpedo gun boat. 1904: b/u.

1892 *9 de Julio*, Argentinian cruiser. c.1930: b/u.

1892 *Tiradentes*, Brazilian gunboat. Laid down as *Republica*. c.1920: b/u.

1892 *Republica*, Brazilian cruiser. Laid down as *15 de Novembro*. c.1928: Discarded.

1892 *Yoshino*, Japanese cruiser. 1904: Sank following collision.

1893 *Blanco Encalada*, Chilean cruiser. c.1946: Discarded.

1894 *Tatsuta*, Japanese torpedo boat destroyer. 1918: Submarine depot ship, r/n *Nagaura Maru*. 1926: Removed from effective list.

1895 *Swordfish*, British torpedo boat destroyer. 1910: b/u.

1895 *Buenos Aires*, Argentinian cruiser. 1931: b/u.

1895 *Spitfire*, British torpedo boat destroyer. 1912: b/u.

1896 *Pactolus*, British cruiser. 1921: b/u.

1896 *Ministro Zenteno*, Chilean cruiser. c.1931: b/u.

1896 *Esmeralda*, Chilean cruiser. c.1932: b/u.

1896 *Yashima*, Japanese battleship. 1904: Struck mine and foundered during Russo-Japanese War.

1896 *Barroso*, Brazilian cruiser. c.1931: discarded.

1896 *Amazonas*, Brazilian cruiser. 1898: r/n *New Orleans* (USA). 1930: b/u.

1897 *General O'Higgins*, Chilean cruiser. c.1946: b/u.

1897 *Hai Tien*, Chinese cruiser. 1904: Wrecked 60 miles from Shanghai.

1898 *Don Carlos I*, Portuguese cruiser. 1910: r/n *Almirante Reis*. c.1926: Dismantled.

1898 *General Baquedano*, Chilean sail training ship. c.1958: b/u.

1898 *Tokiwa*, Japanese cruiser. 1945: Sunk by US carrier aircraft. 1946: Salvaged and scrapped.

1898 *Asama*, Japanese cruiser. 1946: b/u.

1899 *Cobra*, British torpedo boat destroyer. 1901: Wrecked in North Sea.

1899 *Capitan Thompson*, Argentinian torpedo boat destroyer. c.1928: Deleted.

1899 *Albany*, American cruiser. 1897: Laid down as *Abreu* (Brazil). 1930: b/u.

1899 *Idzumo*, Japanese cruiser. 1945: Sunk by U.S. carrier aircraft. 1946: Salvaged, scrapped.

1899 *Hatsuse*, Japanese battleship. 1904: Foundered after striking a mine during Russo-Japanese War.

1900 *Eidsvold*, Norwegian coast defence battle ship. 1940: Sunk by German destroyers.

1900 *Iwate*, Japanese cruiser. 1945: Sunk by US carrier aircraft. 1947: Salvaged, scrapped.

1900 *Norge*, Norwegian coast defence battleship. 1940: Sunk by German destroyers.

1902 *Lancaster*, British cruiser. 1920: b/u.

1903 *Erthogroul* Turkish royal yacht. 1959: Reported afloat but dismantled.

1903 *Hampshire*, British cruiser. 1916: Struck mine and sank off Orkney Islands.

1903 *Abdul Hamid*, Turkish cruiser. 1908: r/n *Hamidieh*. 1945: b/u.

1903 *Constitucion*, Chilean battleship. 1903: Sold to Royal Navy, r/n *Swiftsure*. 1920: b/u.

1903 *Seughudlu*, Turkish state barge.

1903 *Amethyst*, British cruiser. 1920: b/u.

1904 *Attentive*, British cruiser. 1920: b/u.

1904 *Adventure*, British cruiser. 1920: b/u.

1905 *Achilles*, British cruiser. 1921: b/u.

1905 *Kashima*, Japanese battleship. 1924: b/u.

1907 *Superb*, British battleship. 1922: b/u.

1907 *Afridi*, British torpedo boat destroyer. 1919: b/u.

1907 *Invincible*, British battle cruiser. 1916: Sunk at Battle of Jutland.

1908 *Parana*, Argentinian gunboat. c.1957: b/u.

1908 *Minas Geraes*, Brazilian battleship. 1953: b/u.

1908 *Rosario*, Argentinian gunboat. 1957: b/u.

1909 *Bahia*, Brazilian cruiser. 1945: Lost by explosion off Coast of Brazil.

1909 *Newcastle*, British cruiser. 1923: b/u.

1909 *Rio Grande do Sul*, Brazilian cruiser. c.1950: Deleted.

1910 *Weymouth*, British cruiser. 1928: b/u.

1911 *Chao Ho*, Chinese training cruiser. 1937: Sunk by gunfire from Japanese warship.

1911 *Monarch*, British battleship. 1925: Sunk as target.

1913 *Birmingham*, British cruiser. 1931: b/u.

1913 *Nidaros*, Norwegian coast defence battle ship. 1915: Transferred to Royal Navy, r/n *Gorgon*. 1928: b/u.

1913 *Almirante Latorre*, Chilean battleship. 1911: Laid down as *Valparaiso*. 1914: Transferred to Royal Navy, r/n *Canada*. 1920: Sold to Chile, r/n *Almirante Latorre*. 1958: b/u.

1913 *Rio de Janeiro*, Brazilian battleship. Jan 1914: Sold to Turkey, r/n *Sultan Osman I*. Aug. 1914: Seized in Tyne. Transferred to Royal Navy, r/n *Agincourt*. 1922: b/u.

1914 *W 1*, British submarine. 1916: Transferred to Italy. 1919: b/u.

1914 *Bjorgvin*, Norwegian coast defence battle ship. 1915: Sold to Royal Navy, completed as monitor *Glatton*. 1918: Blown up by accident. 1925: Raised and b/u.

1915 *W 4*, British submarine. 1916: Transferred to Italy. 1917: War loss.

1915 *W 2*, British submarine. 1916: Transferred to Italy. c.1919: b/u.

1915 *W 3*, British submarine. 1916: Transferred to Italy. c.1919: b/u.

1915 *E 30*, British submarine. 1916: Sunk North Sea, cause unknown.

1915 *G 6*, British submarine. 1921: b/u.

1915 *E 29*, British submarine. 1922: b/u.

1916 *K 11*, British submarine. 1921: b/u.

1916 *G 7*, British submarine. 1918: Lost in North Sea, cause unknown.

1917 *K 12*, British submarine. 1926: b/u.

1918 *Eagle*, British aircraft carrier. 1913: Laid down as battleship *Almirante Cochrane* (Chile). 1917: Acquired by Royal Navy. 1942: Torpedoed and sunk by *U-73* in Mediterranean.

MERCHANT VESSELS

1888 *Russian Prince*, British oil tanker. 1911: Belgian owners, r/n *Kasbek*. 1921: Spanish owners, r/n *Eduardo*. 1937: b/u.

1888 *Energie*, German oil tanker. 1914: Bahama owners.1916: British owners, r/n *Artesia*. 1918: Sunk by U-156 in North Atlantic.

1891 *Aral*, British oil tanker. 1929: b/u.

1892 *Restorer*, British cable ship. 1952: b/u.

1901 *Fortunatus*, Australian passenger cargo steamer. 1907: Abandoned on fire when bound Calcutta towards Australia.

1901 *Swazi*, British cargo steamer. 1926: Dutch owners, r/n *Scheldestroomm*. 1933: b/u.

1902 *Lucigen*, British oil tanker. 1907: r/n *Cuyahoga*. 1914: r/n *Massasoit*. 1929: Sold to German owners, r/n *Tageha*. 1931: Sold to Italian owners, r/n *Delia*. 1933: b/u.

In addition to those vessels listed, the Italian torpedo boats *Castore* and *Pollux* were constructed at Elswick, dismantled, then shipped out to Italy in sections for re-erection at Armstrong Whitworth's Pozzuoli Yard. The keel of the Siamese gunboat *Ratanakosindra* was laid down on 28 August 1914, but work on her ceased four months later due to circumstances brought about by the onset of the First World War. She was subsequently dismantled and transferred to the Walker Yard. A number of miscellaneous craft were also built. They included two 738-ton coal haulabouts for the British Admiralty, a 418 ton floating workshop, a 256 ton pontoon for the Mersey Docks and Harbour Board's floating crane *Titan* and several steam launches. Amongst these was the 27 ton *Winifred*, which was used by the yard. She was launched in 1886 by the three-year-old daughter of Sir William White.

SOME SOURCES CONSULTED

PUBLISHED WORKS

Armstrong Mitchell & Co. *Programme of Visit to the Works of Sir William Armstrong* (Newcastle, 1886)

Colledge, J.J. *Ships of the Royal Navy*, Vol 1 (Newton Abbot, 1969)

Greger, R. *Austro-Hungarian Warships of World War I* (Shepperton, 1976)

Haigh, K.R. *Cableships and Submarine Cables*, 2nd ed. (Greenwich,1978)

Hocking, C. *Dictionary of Disasters at Sea During the Age of Steam* (London, 1969)

Jentschura, H., D. Jung, P. Mickel, *Warships of the Imperial Japanese Navy*, 1869-1945 (London, 1977)

Kemp, P. Ed. *The Oxford Companion to Ships and the Sea* (London, 1976)

Le Fleming, H.M. *Warships of World War I* (London, c1960)

Lloyds of London *Lloyds' War Losses – The First World War* (London, 1990)

Marsh, E.J. *British Destroyers* (London, 1966)

Schell, W.A. compiler, *Register of Merchant Vessels completed 1890-1904* (Lyndoch, Australia, 1988-1990)

Tennent, A.J. *British Merchant Ships Sunk by U-Boats in the 1914-1918 War* (Newport, Gwent, 1990)

U.S. Naval History Division *American Naval Fighting Ships*, Vols 1-8 (Washington, 1959-1981)

NEWSPAPERS

Illustrated Chronicle (Newcastle)

Newcastle Daily Chronicle

Newcastle Daily Journal

The Times

PERIODICALS

Marine News

The Mariner

Sea Breezes

Ship Building and Shipping Record

The Shipbuilder

Warship International (Particularly a series of articles by P. Brook: *The Elswick Cruisers* [1970-1971])

REGISTERS AND ANNUAL PUBLICATIONS

Janes Fighting Ships

Lloyds' Register of Shipping

Mercantile Navy List & Maritime Directory

UNPUBLISHED MS

Brook, P. *Elswick Cruisers*, 1948 (held by Newcastle City Libraries)